The Seagull Sartre Library

✳

The Seagull Sartre Library

The Seagull Sartre Library

VOLUME 8
ON CAMUS

JEAN-PAUL SARTRE

TRANSLATED BY
CHRIS TURNER

LONDON NEW YORK CALCUTTA

This work is published with the support of
Institut français en Inde – Embassy of France in India

❊

Seagull Books, 2021

Originally published in Jean-Paul Sartre,
Situations I © Éditions Gallimard, Paris, 1947, and
Situations IV © Éditions Gallimard, Paris, 1964

These essays were first published in English translation
by Seagull Books in *Portraits* (2009) and *Critical Essays* (2010)

English translation © Chris Turner, 2009, 2010

ISBN 978 0 8574 2 911 7

British Library Cataloguing-in-Publication Data
A catalogue record for this book is available
from the British Library

Typeset by Seagull Books, Calcutta, India
Printed and bound by Hyam Enterprises, Calcutta, India

CONTENTS

✳

REPLY TO ALBERT CAMUS[1]

My dear Camus,

Our friendship was not easy, but I shall miss it. If today
you break it off, doubtless that means it would inevitably
have ended some day. Many things brought us together,
few separated us. But those few were still too many:
friendship, too, tends to become totalitarian; there has
to be agreement on everything or a quarrel, and those
who don't belong to any party themselves behave like
members of imaginary parties. I shall not carp at this: it
is as it must be. But, for just this reason, I would have
preferred our current disagreement to be over matters of
substance and that there should not be a whiff of
wounded vanity mingled with it. Who would have said,
who would have believed that everything would end
between us in an authors' quarrel in which you played

1 This was written in response to Albert Camus, 'Lettre au directeur
des *Temps Modernes*', *Les Temps modernes*, 82 (August 1952). [Trans.]

Trissotin to my Vadius?[2] I did not want to reply to you. Who would I be convincing? Your enemies, certainly, and perhaps my friends? And you—who do you think you are convincing? Your friends and my enemies. To our common enemies, who are legion, we shall both give much cause for laughter. That much is certain.

Unfortunately, you attacked me so deliberately and in such an unpleasant tone that I cannot remain silent without losing face. I shall, therefore, reply: without anger but, for the first time since I've known you, without mincing my words. A mix of melancholy conceit and vulnerability on your part has always deterred people from telling you unvarnished truths. The result is that you have fallen prey to a gloomy immoderation that conceals your inner difficulties and which you refer to, I believe, as Mediterranean moderation. Sooner or later, someone would have told you this, so it might as well be me. But do not fear, I shall not attempt your portrait; I do not want to incur the criticism you gratuitously level at Jeanson: I shall speak of your letter and of it alone, with a few references to your works if necessary.

It amply suffices to show—if I must speak of you the way the anti-Communist speaks of the USSR; alas,

2 Characters from Molière's play *Les femmes savantes* [The Learned Ladies, 1672]. Trissotin is described as a wit, Vadius as a classical scholar; they quarrel over the quality of Trissotin's poetry. Sartre's 'Who would have said, who would have believed' here is also a clear reference to the well-known exchange between Rodrigue and Chimène in Act III, Scene 4 of Cornielle's *Le Cid*. [Trans.]

the way *you* speak of it—that you have carried through your Thermidorian Reaction. Where is Meursault, Camus? Where is Sisyphus? Where today are those Trotskyites of the heart who preached permanent revolution? Murdered, no doubt, or in exile. A violent, ceremonious dictatorship has established itself within you, basing itself on a fleshless bureaucracy and claiming to enforce the moral law. You wrote that my collaborator 'would like us to rebel against everything except the Communist party and state', but I fear, in my turn, that you rebel more easily against the Communist state than against yourself. It seems that the concern in your letter is to place yourself, *as quickly as possible*, beyond debate. You tell us this in the very first lines: it is not your intention to discuss the criticisms made of you, nor to argue with your adversary as an equal. Your aim is to *teach*. With the praiseworthy, didactic concern to edify the readers of the *Temps modernes*, you take Jeanson's article, which you assume to be symptomatic of the evil gnawing away at our societies and make it the subject of a lecture on pathology. It is as though we were in Rembrandt's painting, with you as the doctor and Jeanson the corpse, and you were pointing out his wounds to the astonished public. For it is of no matter to you at all, is it, that the offending article discusses your book? Your book is not at issue; a God guarantees its value. It will merely serve as a touchstone for revealing the guilty man's bad faith. In doing us the honour of participating in this issue of *Les Temps modernes*, you bring a portable pedestal with you. Admittedly, you do change method part way through and abandon your professorial demonstration and your 'tense serenity' to launch a vehement attack on me. But you were careful to say you were not defending your cause: what would be the point? Only Jeanson's criticisms—so tendentious that they leave you unscathed—run the risk of infringing inviolable principles and offending venerable personalities. It is these persons and principles you are defending: 'It is not me . . . he has treated unfairly, but our reasons for living and struggling and the legitimate hope we have of overcoming our contradictions. In the event, silence was no longer an option.'

But tell me, Camus, by what mystery can your works not be discussed without removing humanity's reasons for living? By what miracle do the objections made against you turn all at once into sacrilege? When *Passage du Malin* received the reception it did, I don't remember François Mauriac writing to *Le Figaro* to say the critics had imperilled the Catholic faith.[3] The fact is that you have a mandate: you speak, you say, 'in the name of that poverty that produces thousands of advocates and never a single brother'. If this is the case, we have to throw in the towel: if it is true that poverty came to you and said, 'Go and speak in my name,' we cannot but be silent and listen to its voice. Only I admit I don't follow your thinking very clearly: you speak in its name, but are you its

---

3 Literally, 'passage of evil'. The great Catholic writer's third play—published by La Table ronde, Paris, 1948, and staged the same year—was a resounding critical failure. [Trans.]

advocate, its brother or its brother advocate? And if you are a brother to the poor, how did you become one? Since it cannot be by ties of blood, it must be a matter of the heart. But no, this cannot be either, since you *are selective about* your poor—I don't think you are a brother to the unemployed Communist in Bologna or the wretched day-labourer struggling against Bao-Dai and the colonialists in Indochina. Did you become a brother to the poor by your condition? You may have been so once but you are no longer; you are middle-class, like Jeanson and me. Is it by devotion, then? But if that devotion is intermittent, how close we are here to the lady bountiful and her charity. And if, to dare to call oneself a brother to the wretched, one must devote every moment of one's life to them, then you are not their brother: whatever your concern, it is not your sole motive and you don't greatly resemble Saint Vincent de Paul or a 'little sister of the poor'. Their brother? No. You are an advocate who says, 'These are my brothers' because these are the words most likely to move the jury to tears. You'll appreciate that I've heard too many paternalistic speeches: permit me to distrust that kind of brotherliness. And poverty did not give you any message. I have not the slightest intention, I assure you, of denying you the right to speak of it. But if you do, let it be, like us, at your own risk, accepting in advance the possibility of disavowal.[4]

---

4 You must have formed the habit of projecting the failings of your thought on to others to believe that Jeanson claimed to speak in the name of the proletariat.

But what does all this matter to you? If we take the poor away from you, you will still have plenty of allies. The former Resistance fighters, for example. Jeanson, poor man, did not remotely intend to offend them. He merely wanted to say that French people of our kind were faced with a political choice in 1940 (for we were of the same kind then: the same educational background, principles and interests). He was not claiming that resistance would have been easy; and, though he had not yet had the benefit of your lessons, he was not unaware of torture, shootings and deportations, nor of the reprisals that followed resistance attacks and the excruciating dilemmas of conscience they posed for some. He had been told of these things, you may rest assured. But these difficulties emerged out of action itself; to know them, one had already to have committed oneself. If he remains convinced that the decision to resist was not difficult to *make*, he is in no doubt either that it took great physical and moral courage to *sustain* it. Yet, he suddenly saw you appealing to the Resistance and—I blush here on your behalf—invoking the dead. 'He does not necessarily understand that the Resistance . . . never seemed to me either a happy or an easy form of history, any more than it did to any of those who really suffered from it, who killed or died in it.'

No, he does not necessarily understand that: he wasn't in France at the time but in a Spanish concentration camp, a result of trying to join the *armée d'Afrique*. But let us put these badges of honour aside. If Jeanson had lost an arm in the camp in which he almost died, his article would be neither better nor worse than it is. *The Rebel*[5] would be neither better nor worse if you hadn't joined the Resistance or had been sent to a concentration camp.

But here is another protestor. Jeanson—rightly or wrongly, I shall not get involved—criticized you for a certain ineffectiveness of thought. Immediately summoned up, the old political activist comes on stage: he is the offended party. You, however, confine yourself to gesturing towards him and informing us that you are tired. Tired of receiving lessons in efficacity, admittedly, but, *above all*, tired of seeing them given to mature family men by young upstarts. To this, one might, of course, reply that Jeanson was not speaking about political activists, young or old, but that he ventured, as is his right, an appreciation of that henceforth *historical* reality termed revolutionary syndicalism—for one may judge a movement ineffective while at the same time admiring the courage, spirit of enterprise, self-denial, even efficiency, of those who took part in it. Above all, one might reply that he was speaking about *you* who are not a political activist.

What if I were to quote an old Communist activist to you, after making him rich in years and loading him

---

5 Albert Camus, *L'Homme révolté* (Paris: Gallimard, 1951); *The Rebel: An Essay on Man in Revolt* (Anthony Bower trans.) (London: Hamish Hamilton, 1953). [Trans.]

down with the ills best calculated to evoke emotional effect? What if I brought him on stage and had him make the following comments:

> I'm tired of seeing bourgeois like you bent on destroying the Party that is my one hope when they are incapable of putting anything in its place. I don't say the Party is above criticism; I do say you have to earn the right to criticize it. I have no truck with your moderation, Mediterranean or otherwise, and even less with your Scandinavian republics. Our hopes are not yours. And you may perhaps be my brother— fraternity costs so little—but certainly not my comrade.

What emotion, eh? I've trumped your activist with an activist-and-a-half. And we would lean, you and I, on the struts that hold up the scenery, receiving the applause of the public, each overcome by a healthy tiredness. But you know very well I do not play that particular game: I have never spoken except in my own name. And then, if I were tired, it seems to me I would be rather ashamed to say so: there are so many people who are more tired. If we are tired, Camus, let's go and rest, since we have the means to. But let us not hope to shake the world by compelling it to take stock of our weariness.

What name am I to give to these manoeuvres? Intimidation? Blackmail? At the very least, their aim is to terrorize: the unfortunate critic, surrounded all of a sudden by this host of heroes and martyrs, ends up jumping to attention like a civilian lost among soldiers. But what a confidence trick! Are you really asking us to believe they have lined up behind you? Nonsense, it is you who have put yourself at their head. Have you changed, then, so much? You used to condemn the use of violence everywhere and now, in the name of morality, you subject us to virtuous violence; you used to be the first servant of your moralism and now you are making it serve you.

What is disconcerting in your letter is that it is too '*written*'. I have no quarrel with its ceremoniousness, which comes naturally to you, but I object to the ease with which you wield your indignation. I recognize that our age has its unpleasant aspects and that it must at times be a relief, for red-blooded natures, to bang on the table and shout. But I regret the fact that upon this disorder of the mind, for which there may well be excuses, you have based a rhetorical order. One is not as ready to show indulgence to controlled violence as to the involuntary kind. With what cunning you play the cool customer, so that your outbursts will astonish us the more; how artfully you let your anger show through, only to conceal it immediately beneath a smile that seeks to be falsely reassuring! Is it my fault if these techniques remind me of the law courts! Only the Public Prosecutor knows how to affect irritation at the opportune moment, to retain control of his anger even in the wildest outbursts and to switch, if need be, to a burst of 'hearts and flowers'. Wouldn't the Republic of the Well-Meaning have appointed you its Public Accuser?[6]

I am here pulled aside and advised not to accord too much importance to stylistic devices. I would willingly give in, only it is difficult in this letter to distinguish devices in general from bad devices. You call me Mr Editor, when each of us knows we have been friends for ten years: this is, I agree, merely a device; you address yourself to me when your clear intention is to refute Jeanson: this is a bad device. Is it not your aim to transform your critic into an *object*, into a dead man? You speak *of him* as though of a soup-tureen or a mandolin; you never speak *to him*. This indicates that he has placed himself beyond the bounds of the human: by your good offices, the resistance fighters, the prisoners, the activists and the poor turn him to stone. At times you succeed in annihilating him altogether, calmly writing '*your* article', as though I were its author. This isn't the first time you have used this trick: Hervé attacked you in a Communist journal and someone mentioned his article in *L'Observateur*, describing it as 'noteworthy' but offering no further comment. You asked the editor of that periodical how he could justify the adjective employed by his colleague and explained at length why Hervé's article was

---

6 *Accusateur public*: the Prosecutor of the French Revolutionary Tribunal. [Trans.]

anything but 'noteworthy'. In short, you responded to Hervé but without addressing yourself to him: does one speak to a Communist? But I ask you, Camus, *who* are you to assume such a lofty stance? And what gives you the right to affect a superiority over Jeanson that *no one* grants you? Your literary merits are not in question; it matters little that you are the better writer and he the better thinker, or the other way about: the superiority you accord yourself, which gives you the right not to treat Jeanson as a human being, must be a *racial* superiority. Has Jeanson, by his criticisms, perhaps indicated that he differs from you in the way ants differ from human beings? Is there, perhaps, a racism of moral beauty? You have a handsome spirit and his is ugly: communication is not possible between you. And it is here that the device becomes intolerable because, to justify your attitude, you have to discover some blackness in his soul. And to discover it, isn't the easiest method first to put it there? For, what is this about? Jeanson didn't like your book. He said so and you didn't like it: so far, then, nothing exceptional. You wrote to criticize his criticism: you cannot be blamed for this; Monsieur de Montherlant does it every day.[7] You could go much further. You could say he had not understood a word and that I was a blockhead. You could cast aspersions on the intelligence of the whole editorial board of *Les Temps modernes*: all's fair in love and war. But when you write,

---

7 Henry de Montherlant (1896–1972): novelist, playwright and essayist. [Trans.]

'Your collaborator would like us to rebel against everything except the Communist party and state,' I confess
I feel uneasy: I thought I was faced with a man of letters
and I am, in fact, dealing with an investigating magistrate handling the case on the basis of tendentious police
reports. And if only you would be happy just to call him
a 'Communist mole', but you have to make him a liar
and a traitor: 'The author *has pretended* to mistake what
he has read . . . I found (in the article) neither generosity
nor honesty, but the *futile desire to misrepresent* a position
he could not express without putting himself in a situation where he would have to debate it properly.' You pro-
pose to reveal the (evidently hidden) 'intention' that
leads him to 'practice omission and traduce the book's
argument . . . to make you say the sky is black when you
say it is blue, etc.', to avoid the real problems, to conceal
from the whole of France the existence of Russian concentration camps which your book revealed. What
intention? Well, let's take a look! The intention to show
that any idea that is not Marxist is reactionary. And why,
when all is said and done, does he do that? Here you are
a little less clear-cut, but, if I understand you aright, this
shameful Marxist is afraid of the light. He was attempting with his clumsy hands to stop up all the openings of
your thought, to halt the blinding rays of the obvious.
For, if he had understood you fully, he *could no longer*
call himself a Marxist. The unfortunate man believed it
permissible to be both Communist and bourgeois: he
was hedging his bets. You show him that he must choose:

join the Party or become bourgeois like you.[8] But that is precisely what he will not see. Here, then, are the findings of the investigation: criminal intent, deliberate misrepresentation of another's thought, bad faith, repeated lies. You can no doubt imagine the mixture of stupefaction and merriment with which those who know Jeanson and Jeanson's sincerity, uprightness, scruples and concern for the truth, will greet this charge-sheet.

But what will be most appreciated, I suspect, is the passage in your letter when you invite us to come clean: 'I would find it normal and almost courageous if, tackling this problem openly, you were to justify the existence of these camps. What is abnormal and betrays embarrassment is that you do not mention them at all.' Here we are at police headquarters, the cop is pacing up and down and his shoes are squeaking, as they do in the cinema: 'We know the whole story, I tell you. Saying nothing isn't helping your case. Come on, admit you were involved. You knew these camps, didn't you? Just say you did and it will all be over. The court will take a favourable view of your confession.' In heaven's name, Camus, how *serious* you are and, to employ one of your own words, how frivolous! And what if you were wrong? What if your book merely revealed your philosophical incompetence? What if it were put together from second-hand information, hastily cobbled together? What if it merely afforded the privileged a good conscience, as

8 For you are bourgeois, Camus, like me; what else could you be?

might be attested by the critic who wrote the other day, 'With Monsieur Camus, revolt is changing sides'? And what if your reasoning were not so very correct? If your ideas were vague and banal? And if Jeanson had quite simply been struck by the indigence of those ideas? If, far from obscuring your radiantly plain facts, he had been forced to light lanterns to make out the contours of weak, obscure, garbled ideas? I do not say that this is the case, but could you not conceive *for one moment* that it might be? Are you so afraid of contradiction? Must you discredit all those who look you in the face as soon as you can? Can you accept only bowed heads? Was it not possible for you to defend your argument and maintain its correctness, while understanding that the other man thought it was wrong? Why do you, who defend *risk* in history, refuse it in literature? Why do you have to be defended by a whole universe of inviolable values instead of fighting against us—or with us—without divine intervention? You once wrote: 'We are stifling among people who believe they are absolutely right, either in their political machines or their ideas.' And it was true. But I'm very much afraid you may have gone over to the side of the stiflers and are abandoning forever your old friends, the stifled.

What really is too much is that you resort to the practice we heard criticized quite recently during a public meeting in which you took part—a practice termed, I believe, *conflation*. In certain political trials, if there are several defendants, the judge combines the charges so as to be able to combine the sentences: of course, this happens only in totalitarian states. Yet this is the procedure you have chosen. From one end of your indictment to the other, you pretend to confuse me with Jeanson. And how do you do this? It is simple, though it needed some thinking out: by an artifice of language, you disorient the reader to the point where he no longer knows which of us you are talking about. Step one: I am the editor of the journal, so it's me you are addressing—an irreproachable procedure. Step two: you invite me to acknowledge I am responsible for the articles published in it—I agree that this is the case. Step three: it *therefore* follows that I approve of Jeanson's attitude and, moving on quickly, that his attitude is also mine. Once this is established, it matters little which of us held the pen—in any event, the article is mine. Skilful use of the personal pronoun will complete the conflation: '*Your* article . . . *You* should have . . . *You* were entitled . . . *You* were not entitled . . . As soon as *you* spoke . . .' Jeanson, you imply, was merely embroidering on a canvas prepared by me. There is a double advantage here: you present him as my scribe and henchman, and there you have your revenge. And, then, here am I, a criminal in my turn: I am the one insulting the activists, the Resistance fighters and the poor; I am the one who covers his ears when the Soviet camps are mentioned; I am the one seeking to hide your light under a bushel. One example will suffice to expose the method here: it will be clear that the 'offence', which loses all substance if ascribed to its true author, turns into a crime when the charge is levelled against the person who did not commit it.

When you write, 'No review of my book can leave aside the fact (of the Russian camps),' you are addressing Jeanson alone. It is the critic you are taking issue with for not speaking, *in his article*, about the concentration camps. Perhaps you are right. Perhaps Jeanson could reply that it is farcical to have the author decide what the critic is to say; moreover, you don't speak much of the camps in your book and it's not easy to see why you suddenly demand their being taken into consideration, unless some poorly primed informers have led you to believe you would thereby be embarrassing us. In any event, this is a legitimate debate that you and Jeanson could have. But when you then write, '*You* retain the relative right to ignore the fact of the camps in the USSR, so long as you do not tackle the questions raised by revolutionary ideology in general and by Marxism in particular, *you* lose it if you tackle those questions, and *you* tackle them *by speaking* about my book,' or alternatively: 'I would find it normal . . . if *you* justified the existence of the camps,' then it is *me* you are addressing. Well, let me reply that these interpellations are deceitful: for you take advantage of the undeniable fact that Jeanson—*as was his right*—did not, in reviewing your book, speak of the Soviet camps, so that you may insinuate that I, the editor of a journal that claims to be politically committed, have never tackled the question—something which, if it were the case, might be said to be a serious offence against honesty. Only it just so happens that it is untrue: a few days after Rousset's declarations, we devoted several articles to the camps, together with an editorial to which I fully subscribed.[9] And, if you compare the dates, you'll see that the issue was put together *before* Rousset's declarations. But that matters little: I merely wanted to show you that we raised the question of the camps and took a stand at the very moment when French public opinion was discovering them. We returned to the subject a few months later *in another editorial* and clarified our point of view in articles and notes. The existence of these camps may enrage and horrify us; it may be that we are obsessed with them, but why should it *embarrass us*? Have I ever backed away when it came to saying what I thought about the Communist attitude? And if I am a 'crypto-communist', a shameful fellow traveller, why do they hate me and not you? But let us not boast about the hatreds we inspire: I will tell you honestly that I deeply regret this hostility; sometimes I might even go so far as to envy the profound indifference they show towards you. But what can I do about it, except precisely no longer say what I believe to be true? What are you claiming then, when you write, 'You retain the relative right to ignore . . .' etc.? Either you are insinuating that Jeanson does not exist and is

---

9 David Rousset, a survivor of Buchenwald, was the first person to bring the Gulag system to light within the French Left. He was denounced by *Les Lettres Françaises* in 1949 as a 'falsifying Trotskyite', but went on to fight a successful libel action against this charge.

one of my pseudonyms, which is absurd, or you are claiming I've never said a word about the camps, which is slanderous. Yes, Camus, like you I find these camps unacceptable, but I also find unacceptable the use the so-called bourgeois press makes of them each day. I do not say that the Madagascan takes precedence over the Turkoman; I say we must not use the sufferings inflicted on the Turkoman to justify those *we* inflict on the Madagascan.

I have seen anti-Communists delight in the existence of these jails, I have seen them use them to salve their consciences; and I did not have the impression they were helping the Turkomans, but, rather, exploiting their misery in the same way as the USSR exploited their labour. We might truly term this full employment for the Turkomans. But let's be serious, Camus: tell me, if you will, what sentiment Rousset's revelations could have stirred in an anti-Communist's heart. Despair? Affliction? Shame at being human? Nonsense. It's difficult for a Frenchman to put himself in the shoes of a Turkoman, to feel sympathy for that abstract being, the Turkoman, when seen from France. At best, I will concede that, among the best of Frenchmen, the memory of the German camps reawakened a kind of very spontaneous horror. And then, of course, fear too. But, don't you see, in the absence of any relationship with the Turkoman, what must provoke indignation, and perhaps despair, was the idea that a socialist government, supported by an army of functionaries, could have systematically reduced human beings to slavery? Now *that,*

Camus, cannot affect the anti-Communist, who *already believed the USSR capable of anything*. The only sentiment this information provoked in him was—and it pains me to say this—*joy*. Joy because he had, at last, his *proof* and that now 'we should really see something'. The point now was to act not on the workers—the anti-Communist isn't so foolish—but on all the good people who remained 'on the Left'; they had to be intimidated, stricken with terror. If they opened their mouths to complain about some outrage, it was closed immediately with a 'What about the camps?' People were *commanded* to denounce the camps on pain of collusion with them. An excellent method, in which the unfortunates either offended the Communists or were made to collude in 'the greatest crime on earth'. It was around this time that I began to find these blackmailers despicable. For, in my view, the scandal of the camps puts us all on our mettle. You as much as me. And everyone else: the Iron Curtain is merely a mirror and the two halves of the world reflect each other. To every turn of the screw *here* there is a corresponding turn *over there*; we both turn the screw and feel its bite. A tougher line in the USA, which expresses itself in a renewed outbreak of witch-hunting,[10] causes a harder line on the part of the Russians, which will perhaps be expressed in increased arms production and a higher number of forced labourers. The opposite may, of course, be true too. Those who condemn today must know that

---

10 Sartre is referring to Senator Joseph McCarthy's anti-Communist campaign of the 1950s. [Trans.]

our situation will force them tomorrow to do worse things than they have condemned; and when I see this joke scrawled on the walls of Paris—'Take your holidays in the USSR, land of liberty' over grey shadowy figures depicted behind bars, it isn't the Russians I find disgusting. Don't misunderstand me, Camus: I know you have on a hundred occasions denounced and fought Franco's tyranny or the colonial policy of our government with all the powers available to you; you have won the *relative* right to speak of the Soviet concentration camps. But I shall make two criticisms of your position: you were fully entitled to mention the camps in a serious work, the aim of which is to provide us with an explanation of our times; indeed, it was your *duty*; what seems unacceptable to me is that you use this today as a piece of clap-trap and that you, like the others, exploit the Turkoman and the Kurd the more surely to crush a critic who did not praise you.

And then I'm sorry you produce your sledgehammer argument to justify a quietism that refuses to distinguish between the different masters. For, as you say yourself, it is the same thing to treat all masters as the same as to treat all slaves as the same. And if you do not make any distinction between slaves, you condemn yourself to have only a theoretical sympathy for them. Particularly as it often happens that the 'slave' is the ally of those you call the masters. This explains the embarrassment you get into over the war in Indochina. If we are to apply your principles, then the Vietnamese have been colonized and hence are slaves, but they are Communists and hence are tyrants. You criticize the European proletariat for not having publicly expressed disapproval of the Soviets, but you also criticize the governments of Europe because they are going to admit Spain into UNESCO; in this case I can see only one solution for you: the Galapagos Islands. It seems to me, by contrast, that the only way to help the slaves over there is to take the side of the slaves over here.

I was going to close on this, but, re-reading your letter, I get the impression that your indictment claims also to take in our ideas.[11] It would seem, in fact, that in employing the words 'unbridled freedom', you have our conception of human freedom in your sights. Should I insult you by believing these to be your words? No, you are incapable of such an error; you have no doubt picked up the words 'unbridled freedom' from the study by Troisfontaines.[12] Well, I shall at least share with Hegel the distinction of not having been read by you. But what a bad habit you have of not going back to sources! Yet *you know very well* that only the real forces of this world can be 'bridled' and that the physical action of an object

---

11 It isn't my place to defend those of Marx, but allow me to tell you that the dilemma into which you have boxed those ideas (either Marx's 'prophecies' are true or Marxism is merely a method) misses the whole of Marxist philosophy and everything in it that constitutes for me (who am not a Marxist) its profound truth.

12 This is a reference to Roger Troisfontaines, *Le Choix de Jean-Paul Sartre. Exposé et critique de 'L'Etre et le Néant'* (Paris: Montaigne, 1945). [Trans.]

is restrained by acting on one of the factors affecting it. But freedom is not a force: this is not my decision; it is part of its very definition. Freedom either exists or does not, but, if it does, it lies outside the sequence of cause and effect; it is of another order. Would you not laugh if we spoke of Epicurus' unrestrained *clinamen*? Since that philosopher, the conception of determinism and, as a consequence, of freedom has become a little more complicated, but the idea of a break, a disconnection or 'solution of continuity' remains. I hardly dare advise you to refer here to *Being and Nothingness*;[13] to read it would seem to you pointlessly arduous: you detest difficulties of thought and are quick to decree that there is nothing to understand, so as to avoid in advance the criticism that you have not understood. The fact remains that in that book I explained precisely the conditions for this break. And if you had spent a few minutes reflecting on someone else's ideas, you would have seen that freedom cannot be restrained or bridled: it has neither wheels nor legs, nor jaws between which to put a bridle, and, since it is determined by the undertaking in which it is involved, it finds its limits in the positive, but necessarily *finite,* character of that undertaking.

We are on a journey, we have to choose: the *project* brings its own enlightenment and gives the situation its

13 Jean-Paul Sartre, *Being and Nothingness: An Essay on Phenomenological Ontology* (Hazel E. Barnes trans.) (New York: Methuen and Co., 1957) [*L'Être et le néant: Essai d'ontologie phénoménologique* (Paris: Gallimard, 1943)—Trans.]

meaning, but, by the same token, it is merely one particular way of transcending that situation—of understanding it. Our project is ourselves: in the light of it, our relation to the world becomes clearer; the goals and the tools appear that reflect back to us both the world's hostility and our own aim. Having said this, you are quite at liberty to term 'unbridled' the freedom that can alone ground *your own demands*, Camus (for if human beings are not free, how can they 'demand to have a meaning'? Only, you don't like to think about that.). But there will be no more sense to this than if you spoke of oesophagus-less freedom or freedom without hydrochloric acid, and you merely have revealed that, like so many, you confuse politics and philosophy. Unbridled: of course. Without police or magistracy. If we grant the freedom to consume alcoholic drink without setting limits, what will become of the virtuous wife of the drunkard? But French Revolutionary thinking is clearer on this than yours: the limit of one right (i.e. of one freedom) is another right (i.e. another freedom) and not some 'human nature' or other; for nature, whether 'human' or not, can crush human beings but it cannot reduce them to the status of object; if man is an object, he is so for another man. And it is these two ideas—which are, I agree, difficult—that man is free and man is the being by which man becomes an object, that define our present status and enable us to understand *oppression*.

You had believed—on whose authority?—that I first ascribed a paradisiacal freedom to my fellow creatures so as subsequently to clap them in irons. I am so far from this conception that I see around me only freedoms *already enslaved*, attempting to wrest themselves from their *congenital* slavery. Our freedom today is merely *the free choice to struggle to become free*. And the paradoxical aspect of this formula encapsulates the paradox of our *historical* condition. It is not a question, as you see, of *caging* my contemporaries: they are already in the cage; it is a matter, rather, of uniting with them to break down the bars.

For we too, Camus, are committed, and if you really want to prevent a popular movement from degenerating into tyranny, don't begin by condemning it out of hand and threatening to withdraw into the desert, particularly as your deserts are only ever a less frequented part of our cage. To earn the right to influence human beings in struggle, you have first to take part in their fight; you have first to accept a lot of things if you want to try to change a small number. 'History' presents few more desperate situations than ours—this is what excuses the pompous prophecies. But when a man sees the present struggles merely as the imbecilic duel between two equally despicable monsters, I contend that that man has already left us: he has gone off alone to his corner and is sulking; far from seeming to me loftily to judge and dominate an age on which he deliberately turns his back, I see him as entirely conditioned by it and clinging obstinately to the refusal inspired in him by a very historical *ressentiment*. You pity me for having a bad conscience and that is not the case, but, even if I were entirely poisoned by shame, I would feel less alienated and more open than you: for, to keep your conscience in good order you need to condemn; you need a guilty party: if not yourself, then the universe. You pronounce your verdicts and the world responds with not a word; but your condemnations cancel themselves out on contact with it and you have perpetually to begin again. If you stopped, you might see yourself; you have condemned yourself to condemn, Sisyphus.

For us you were—and can again be tomorrow—the admirable conjunction of a person, an action and a body of writings. That was in 1945: we discovered Camus, the Resistance fighter, as we had discovered Camus, the author of *The Outsider*.[14] And when we compared the editor of the underground *Combat* with that Meursault who carried honesty to the point of refusing to say that he loved either his mother or his mistress and whom our society condemned to death, when we knew, above all, that you had not stopped being either of these, the apparent contradiction increased our knowledge of ourselves and the world, and you were little short of exemplary. For you summed up the conflicts of the age in yourself and transcended them through your fiery determination to live them out. You were a *person*, the most complex and richest of persons: the latest and timeliest of the heirs of

---

14 Albert Camus, *L'Étranger* (Paris: Gallimard, 1942); *The Outsider* (Stuart Gilbert trans.) (London: Hamish Hamilton, 1946). [Trans.]

Chateaubriand and the resolute defender of a social cause. You had every good fortune and all the qualities, since you combined a sense of greatness with a passionate taste for beauty, a *joie de vivre* with an awareness of death. Even before the war, and against the bitter experience of what you call the *absurd*, you had chosen to defend yourself by scorn, but you were of the opinion that 'every negation contains a flowering of *yeses*' and you tried to find the consent that underlay every rejection, 'to hallow the accord between love and revolt'. In your view, man is only entirely himself when he is happy. And 'what is happiness but the simple accord between a being and the existence he leads. And what more legitimate accord can bind man to life than the twofold consciousness of his desire to endure and his mortal destiny?' Happiness was neither entirely a state nor entirely an act, but that tension between the forces of death and the forces of life, between acceptance and refusal, by which man defines the *present*—that is to say, both the moment and eternity—and turns into himself. Thus, when you described one of those privileged moments that achieve a temporary accord between man and nature and which, from Rousseau to Breton, have provided our literature with one of its major themes, you were able to introduce into it an entirely new note of *morality*. To be happy is to do one's job as a human being; you showed us 'the duty of being happy'. And that duty merged with the affirmation that man is the only being in the world who has a meaning, 'because he is the only creature to demand that he should'. The experience of happiness, similar to Bataille's 'Torment',[15] but richer and more complex, made you stand up to an absent God as a reproach but also as a challenge: 'Man must affirm justice in order to combat eternal injustice, and create happiness to protest against the universe of misery.' The universe of misery is not *social* or, at least, not primarily so: it is indifferent, empty Nature, in which man is alien and condemned to die; in a word, it is 'the eternal silence of the Divinity'. So your experience closely combined the ephemeral and the permanent. Aware of being perishable, you wanted to deal only with truths 'that must necessarily rot'. Your body was one of those. You rejected the fraudulence of the Soul and the Idea. But since, in your own words, injustice is *eternal*—that is to say, since the absence of God is a constant throughout the changing course of history—the immediate relation, begun ever anew, of the man who demands that he *have* a meaning (that is to say, demands to be given one) to this God who eternally remains silent, is itself transcendent with respect to history. The tension by which man realizes himself—which is, at the same time, intuitive enjoyment of being—is, therefore, a veritable conversion that wrests him from daily 'agitation' and 'historicity' and reconciles him at last with his condition. We can go no further; no progress can have its place in this instantaneous tragedy. As an Absurdist *avant la lettre*, Mallarmé

---

15 Georges Bataille, 'Le Supplice', in *L'Expérience Intérieure* (Paris: Gallimard, 1943). [Trans.]

wrote: '(The drama) is resolved immediately in the time it takes to show the defeat that occurs with lightning speed' and he seems to me to have provided in advance the key to your theatrical works when he writes: 'The Hero *releases*—the (maternal) hymn that creates him and is restored in the Theatre which this was—from the Mystery in which that hymn was shrouded.'[16] In short, you remain within our great classical tradition which, since Descartes and with the exception of Pascal, is entirely hostile to history. But you, at last, achieved the synthesis between aesthetic pleasure, desire, happiness and heroism, between satisfied contemplation and duty, between Gidean plenitude and Baudelairean dissatisfaction. You topped off Ménalque's immoralism[17] with an austere moralism; the content was not changed.

> There is only one love in this world. Embracing a woman's body also means holding in your arms this strange joy which descends from sky to sea. In a moment, when I throw myself down among the wormwood plants to bring their

16 My translation of part of an enigmatic fragment from Stéphane Mallarmé, 'Igitur', in *Œuvres complètes* (Henri Mondor and G. Jean-Aubry eds) (Paris: Gallimard, 1945), p. 428. [Trans.]

17 Ménalque, like the Nathanael mentioned below, is a character in André Gide's *Les Nourritures terrestres* [1897; *The Fruits of the Earth* (Dorothy Bussy trans.) (New York: Alfred A. Knopf, 1949)], who reappears in *L'Immoraliste* [1902; *The Immoralist* (Dorothy Bussy trans.) (New York: Alfred A. Knopf, 1930)]. It has sometimes been suggested that Ménalque was based on Oscar Wilde, but André Maurois says Gide personally rejected this suggestion. [Trans.]

scent into my body, I shall know, whatever prej-
udice may say, that I am fulfilling a truth which
is that of the sun and which will also be that of
my death.[18]

But since this truth belongs to everyone, since its
extreme singularity is precisely what makes it universal,
since you were breaking open the shell of the pure
present in which Nathanael[19] seeks God and opening it
to the 'profundity of the world', that is to say, to death,
then at the end of this sombre, solitary pleasure, you
rediscovered the universality of an ethics and human
solidarity. Nathanael is no longer alone; he is 'conscious
and proud of sharing' this love of life, stronger than
death, 'with a whole race'. It all ends badly, of course:
the world swallows up the irreconciled libertine. And
you liked to cite this passage from *Obermann*: 'Let us go
down resisting, and if nothingness is to be our fate, let
it not be a just one.'[20]

You do not deny it then. You did not reject history
because you have suffered from it and discovered its
face to be horrendous. You rejected it before you had
any experience of it, because our culture rejects it and
because you located human values in man's struggle

---

18 Albert Camus, 'Nuptials at Tipasa', in *Selected Essays and Notebooks*
(Philip Thody ed. and trans.) (Harmondsworth: Penguin, 1967),
pp. 71–2 (translation modified). [Trans.]

19 See note 3. [Trans.]

20 The epistolary novel *Obermann* was written by Étienne Pivet de
Sénancour in 1804. [Trans.]

'against heaven'. You chose and created yourself as you are by meditating on the misfortunes and anxieties that fell to you personally, and the solution you found for them is a bitter wisdom that strives to deny time.

However, with the coming of war you devoted yourself unreservedly to the Resistance; you fought an austere fight that offered no fame or elevation; the dangers incurred hardly brought one any glory: worse, one ran the risk of being demeaned and debased. That effort, always painful and often solitary, *necessarily* presented itself as a *duty*. And your first contact with history assumed for you the aspect of *sacrifice*. You wrote as much, in fact, and you have said that you were fighting 'for that nuance that separates sacrifice from mysticism.' Don't misunderstand me: if I say 'your first contact with history', it is not to imply that I had another and that it was better. Around that time, we intellectuals had only that contact; and if I refer to it as *yours*, it is because you experienced it more deeply and totally than many of us, myself included. The fact remains that the circumstances of this battle entrenched you in the belief that one must sometimes pay one's tribute to history to have the right, later on, to return to the real duties. You accused the Germans of tearing you away from your battle with heaven to force you to take part in the temporal combats of men: 'For so many years you have tried to *bring me into history.*' And, further on, you write: 'You did the necessary, *we entered history*; and for five years, it was no longer possible to enjoy birdsong.'[21] The history in question was the war; for you that was *other people's madness*. It does not create, it destroys: it prevents the grass from growing, the birds from singing and human beings from making love. It so happened, in fact, that external circumstances seemed to confirm your point of view: *in peacetime* you were fighting a timeless battle against the injustice of our destiny and the Nazis had, in your view, sided with that injustice. In collusion with the blind forces of the universe, they were trying to destroy humanity. You fought, as you put it, 'to save the *idea* of mankind'.[22] In short, it was not your intention to 'make history', as Marx says, but to prevent it from being made. Proof lies in the fact that, after the war, you merely had in mind a return of the *status quo ante*: 'Our condition [continued to be] desperate.' The meaning of the Allied victory seemed to you to be 'the acquisition of two or three nuances that will perhaps have no other use than to help some of us to die better'.

After serving your five years with history, you thought you (and the whole of humanity with you) could return to the despair in which man must find his happiness, and go back to 'proving that we did not deserve so

21 *Lettres à un ami allemand*, my emphasis, J-P. S. [1945; published for the first time in English as 'Letters to a German Friend', in *Resistance, Rebellion, and Death* (Justin O'Brien trans.) (New York: Random House, 1961—Trans.]

22 *Lettres à un ami allemand*. [Trans.]

much injustice' (in whose eyes?) by resuming the desperate battle human beings wage 'against their repellent destinies'. How we loved you in those days. We too were neophytes of history and endured it with repugnance, not understanding that the war of 1940 was merely one mode of historicity—neither more nor less so than the years preceding it. When we thought of you, we thought of Malraux's phrase, 'May victory go to those who made war without liking it,' and we felt a little sorry for ourselves as we repeated it; at that time we were under threat, like you and in you, without our realizing it.

It often happens that cultures produce their richest works when they are about to disappear, and those works are the fruits of the lethal marriage of the old values and the new ones that seem to render them fertile but actually kill them off. In the synthesis you were attempting, the happiness and the yea-saying came from our old humanism, but the revolt and the despair were intruders. They came from outside, from an outside where persons unknown looked on at our spiritual festivities with hatred in their eyes. You had borrowed that gaze from them to turn it on our cultural heritage; it was their simple, stark existence that *threw our tranquil pleasures into question*; of course, the defiance of destiny, the revolt against absurdity all came from you or passed through you: but, thirty or forty years earlier, you would have been made to drop these ill-bred ways and would have joined the ranks of the aesthetes or the Church. Your Revolt assumed the importance it did only because it was prompted in you by this obscure crowd: you barely had time to deflect it against the heavens, where it vanished. And the moral demands you brought to light were simply the idealization of very real demands welling up around you that you had seized on. The equilibrium you achieved between these things could happen only once, for a single moment, in a single person: you had had the good fortune that the common struggle against the Germans symbolized for you, and for us, the unity of all human beings against inhuman fate. By choosing injustice, the German had, of his own volition, ranged himself among the blind forces of Nature and you were able, in *The Plague*,[23] to have his part played by microbes without anyone realizing the mystification. In short, you were, for a few years, the symbol and evidence of solidarity between the classes. This is also what the Resistance seemed to be and it is what you demonstrated in your earliest works: 'Men rediscover their solidarity in order to enter the struggle against their repellent destinies.'

In this way, a combination of circumstances, one of those rare concordances that, for a time, turn a life into the image of a truth, enabled you to conceal from yourself that man's struggle against Nature is both the cause and effect of another struggle, just as old and even more ruthless: the struggle of man against man. You were rebelling against death but, in the belts of iron that ring

---

23 Albert Camus, *La Peste* (Paris: Gallimard, 1947); *The Plague* (Stuart Gilbert trans.) (London: Hamish Hamilton, 1948). [Trans.]

our cities, other people were rebelling against the social conditions that increase the mortality rate. When a child died, you condemned the absurdity of the world and that deaf, blind God you had created so as to be able to spit in His face. But the child's father, if he were a labourer or unemployed, condemned human beings: he knew very well that the absurdity of our condition isn't the same in Passy as it is in Boulogne-Billancourt.[24] And, in the end, the microbes were almost hidden from him by human beings: in the poor districts, the child mortality rate is twice what it is in the wealthy suburbs and, since a different distribution of income could save them,[25] half of the deaths, among the poor, seem like executions, with the microbe merely playing the hangman's final role.

You wanted to achieve—within yourself, through yourself—happiness for everyone by way of a *moral* tension. The sombre masses we were beginning to discover called on us to give up our happiness so that they could become a little less unhappy. Suddenly, the Germans no longer mattered. It was almost as though they had never mattered. We had thought there had been only one way of resisting; we discovered that there were two ways of *seeing* the Resistance. And while you still personified the immediate past for us and were perhaps even the coming

24 Passy is a leafy suburb in the fashionable 16th arrondissement of Paris. Boulogne-Billancourt is a working-class area in that city's Western suburbs. [Trans.]

25 This is not entirely exact. Some are doomed come what may.

man of the near future, for ten million French people who did not recognize their only too real anger in your ideal rebellion, you had already become one of the privileged. The death, life, earth, rebellion and God you spoke of, the 'yes' and the 'no' and the 'love' were, they told you, mere aristocratic amusements. To others, they seemed like something out of a circus. You had written: 'Only one thing is more tragic than suffering and that is the life of a happy man.' And: 'a certain continuity in despair can give birth to joy.' And: 'I was not sure that this splendour of the world was not [the justification] of all men who know that an extreme point of poverty always connects us back to the luxury and riches of the world.'[26] And admittedly, being like you, one of the privileged, I understood what you meant and I believe you have paid your dues to be able to say it. I imagine you have been closer to a certain kind of death and deprivation than many people, and I think you must have known genuine poverty, if not destitution. Coming from your pen, these lines *do not have* the meaning they would in a book by Messrs. Mauriac or Montherlant. Moreover, when you wrote them, they seemed natural. But the key thing today is that *they no longer do*: we know that it takes, if not wealth, then at least culture, the inestimable and unjust riches of culture, to find luxury in the depths of deprivation. One feels that the circumstances

---

26 These three quotations are from Camus, 'Nuptials', in *Selected Essays and Notebooks*, pp. 90, 97, 98 (the translation of the passage cited on p. 97 has been modified). [Trans.]

of your life—even the most painful of them—have chosen you to attest that personal salvation was accessible
to all; and the predominant thought in everyone's heart,
a menacing, hate-filled thought, is that this is possible
only for a few. A hate-filled thought, but what can we
do about that? Hatred gnaws away at everything. Even
in you, who tried not even to hate the Germans, there is
a hatred of God that shows through in your books, and
it has been said that you are even more of an 'anti-theist'
than an atheist. The whole value that oppressed persons
may still have in their own eyes, they put into the hatred
they bear to other human beings. And their friendship
for their comrades also involves the hatred they bear for
their enemies; neither your books nor your example can
do anything for them; you teach an art of living, a 'science of life', you teach us to rediscover our bodies, but
their bodies when they get them back in the evening—
after having them stolen from them all day—are merely
great wretched things that encumber and humiliate
them. These men are *made* by other men; their number
one enemy is man, and, if the strange nature they find
in the factory and the building site still speaks to them
of man, this is because it is men who have transformed
these places into prisons for them.

What options remained open to you? To modify
yourself in part, so as to retain some of your old loyalties,
while satisfying the demands of these oppressed masses.
You would perhaps have done this, had not their repre-
sentatives insulted you, as is their wont. You stopped

dead the slide that was taking place within you and insisted, with renewed defiance, on demonstrating to everyone the union of men in the face of death and the solidarity between classes, when the classes had already resumed their struggles before your very eyes. Thus, what for a time had been an *exemplary reality* became the utterly empty affirmation of an *ideal*—all the more so as this false solidarity had changed into struggle even in your own heart. You found history to be in the wrong and, rather than interpret its course, you preferred to see it as just one more absurdity. Basically, you resumed your initial attitude. You borrowed some sort of idea of the 'divinization of man' from Malraux, Carrouges and twenty other writers and, condemning the human race, you took your stand alongside it, but outside its ranks, like the last of the Mohicans.

Your personality, real and vital so long as it was fed by events, is becoming a mirage. In 1944 it was the future; in 1952 it is the past. And what seems to you the most repellent injustice is that all this is happening to you from outside and without your having changed. It seems to you that the world offers the same riches as it did in the past and that it is human beings who no longer wish to see them. Well, try holding out your hand and you will see if it doesn't all vanish: even Nature has changed its meaning because the relationship of human beings to that Nature has changed. The memories and the language you are left with are increasingly abstract; you are only half living among us and you are tempted to leave us altogether to withdraw into some solitude where you can rediscover the drama that was supposed to be that of mankind and is no longer even your own—in other words, into a society that has remained at a lower level of technical civilization. What is happening to you is, in a sense, quite unjust. But, in another, it is pure justice: you had to change if you wanted to remain yourself and you were afraid of changing. If you find me cruel, have no fear: I shall speak of myself shortly, and in this same tone. There is no point trying to hit back at me; but, trust me, I shall see to it that I pay for all this. For you are absolutely unbearable, but you are, nonetheless, by force of circumstance, my neighbour.

Though engaged, like you, in history, I do not see it as you do. No doubt it has this absurd, fearful countenance for those who view it from Hades: this is because they no longer have anything in common with the human beings who are making it. And if it were a history of ants or bees, I am sure we would see it as a silly, macabre succession of crime, mockery and murder. But if we were ants, perhaps we would take a different view. Until I re-read your *Letters to a German Friend*, I did not understand your dilemma—'Either history has a meaning or it does not,' etc.—but it all became clear to me when I found there this remark which you address to the Nazi soldier, 'For years you have been trying to get me to enter history.' 'Good Lord,' I said to myself, 'since he believes he stands *outside* history, no wonder he lays down his conditions before coming *inside*.' Like a girl testing the water with her toe and asking, 'Is it warm?', you regard history warily. You stick in a finger, then very quickly pull it out again, asking, 'Has it a meaning?' You didn't hesitate in 1941, but then you were being asked to make a sacrifice. It was quite simply a question of preventing the Hitlerian madness from smashing a world where solitary elation was still possible for some, and you were willing to pay the price for your future moments of elation.

Things are different today. It is no longer a question of *defending the status quo* but of changing it. This is something you will agree to only with the firmest of guarantees. And if I thought, as you do, that history is a pool full of mud and blood, I would do as you do, I imagine, and look twice before diving in. But let us suppose that I am already in it; let us suppose that, from my point of view, your very aloofness is proof of your historicity. Suppose you receive the answer Marx would give you: 'History does nothing . . . It is men, real living men who do everything; history is merely the activity of human beings pursuing their own ends.' If this is true, the person who believes he is moving away from history will cease to share his contemporaries' ends and will be sensible only of the absurdity of human restlessness. But if he rails against that restlessness, he will, against his will, re-enter the historical cycle, for he will involuntarily provide the side that is on the ideological defensive (that is to say, the one whose culture is dying) with arguments for discouraging the other. The person who, by contrast, subscribes to the aims of concrete human beings will be forced to choose his friends because, in a society torn apart by civil war, one can neither accept nor reject everyone's aims at the same time. But, as soon as he chooses, everything acquires a meaning: he knows why the enemies resist and why he fights. For only in historical action is the understanding of history vouchsafed. 'Does history have a meaning?' you ask. 'Does it have a purpose?' In my view, it is the question that is meaningless. For history, considered apart from those who make it, is merely an abstract, static concept, and we can neither say that it has a purpose nor that it does not. And the problem is not one of *knowing* its purpose but of *giving* it one.

Moreover, no one acts *solely* with an eye to history. Human beings are, in fact, engaged in short-term projects, lit by distant hopes. And there is nothing absurd about these projects: on the one hand, we have Tunisians rising up against the colonial power, on the other, miners striking for better conditions or on grounds of solidarity. Whether there are values transcendent to history is not the question: we shall merely note that *if there are* such values, they manifest themselves through human actions that are, by definition, historical. And this contradiction is essential to human beings: they become historical through pursuing the eternal, and discover universal values in the concrete action they take to achieve a particular outcome.

If you say this world is unjust, you have lost the game: you are already outside, comparing a justiceless world to a contentless Justice. But you will discover justice in every effort you make to order your undertaking, to divide tasks between your comrades, to submit yourself to discipline or to apply it. And Marx never said history would have an end: how could he have? You might as well say that men would one day have no objectives. He merely spoke of an end to prehistory or, in other words, of an objective that would be achieved within history itself and then left behind, as all objectives are. It is not a matter of establishing whether history has a meaning and whether we deign to participate in it, but, given that we are in it up to our necks, of trying to give it what seems to us the best meaning, by not refusing our participation, no matter how small, in any of the concrete actions that require it.

Terror is an abstract violence. You became terroristic and violent when history—which you rejected—rejected you in turn: this is because you were merely, then, the abstraction of a rebel. Your distrust of human beings led you to presume that any accused person was, *first and foremost*, a guilty one: hence your police methods with Jeanson. Your morality turned first into moralism; today it is merely literature; tomorrow it will perhaps be immorality. What will become of us I do not know: perhaps we shall end up on the same side, perhaps not. The times are hard and confused. In any event, it has been good to be able to tell you what I have been thinking. The review is open to you if you want to reply, but I shall make no further reply to you. I have said what you were for me and what you are at present. But, whatever you may do or say in return, I refuse to fight with you. I hope our silence will lead to this polemic being forgotten.

Les Temps modernes, 82 (August 1952)

＊

ALBERT CAMUS

Six months ago, even yesterday, we were wondering, '*What is he going to do?*' Riven by contradictions we must respect, he had, for the time being, chosen silence. But he was one of those rare men you can happily wait for because they choose slowly and stand by their decisions. One day, he would speak. We would not even have dared to conjecture what he would say. But we thought that he changed with the world, as each of us does: that sufficed for his presence to remain a living one.

We had quarrelled, he and I. A quarrel is nothing—even if you were never to see each other again: it is just another way of living *together*, without losing sight of each other in the narrow, little world allotted to us. This didn't prevent me from thinking of him, from sensing his gaze on the page of the book or the newspaper he was reading and asking myself, 'What's he saying about it, what's he saying about it *right now*?'

His silence which, depending on events and my mood, I thought at times too cautious and, at others, painful, was a quality of each day, like the heat or the light, but a *human* quality. One lived with or against his thought, as revealed to us in his books—*The Fall*,[1] in particular, perhaps the finest and least understood—but always through it. It was a singular adventure of our culture, a movement whose phases and final term one tried to divine.

In this century, and running counter to history, he was the current heir to that long line of moralists whose works perhaps constitute what is most original in French literature. His stubborn humanism, narrow and pure, austere and sensual, fought an uncertain battle against the massive, misshapen events of our times. But, conversely, through the unyielding nature of his refusals, in the heart of our age, against the Machiavellians and the golden calf of realism, he re-asserted the existence of morality.

He *was*, one might almost say, that unshakeable affirmation. If one read or thought, then one ran up against the human values he held in his tightly clenched fist: he called the political act into question. You had either to bypass him or fight him: he was, in a word, indispensable to that tension that constitutes the life of the mind. His very silence in recent years had a positive aspect: this Cartesian of the Absurd refused to leave the

---

1 Albert Camus, *La Chute* (Paris: Gallimard, 1956); *The Fall* (Justin O'Brien trans.) (London: Hamish Hamilton, 1956). [Trans.]

sure ground of morality and tread the uncertain paths
of *practice*. We sensed this, and we sensed also the conflicts on which he remained silent: for morality, taken
on its own, both demands revolt and condemns it.

We were waiting, we had to wait, we had to know;
whatever he might have done or decided subsequently,
Camus would never have ceased to be one of the chief
forces in our cultural field or to represent, in his way, the
history of France and of this century. But we would have
known, perhaps, and understood his itinerary. He had
done everything—produced an entire body of work—
and, as ever, everything still remained to be done. He
said as much: 'My work lies before me.' It is finished.
The particular scandal of this death is the way that the
inhuman has overridden the order of men.

The human order is still merely a disorder: it is
unjust and precarious; people are killed in it, they die of
starvation. But at least it is founded, maintained and
combated by human beings. In that order, Camus
should have lived: this man on the march called us into
question; he was himself a question in search of an
answer; he was living *in the middle of a long life.* For us,
for him, for those who enforce order and those who
reject it, it was important that he end his silence, that he
decide, that he conclude. Others die old; others, under
constant stay of execution, may die at any minute without the meaning of their lives—or *of life*—being
changed. But for us, uncertain and disoriented as we are,

we needed our best men to get to the end of the tunnel. Seldom have the characteristics of a work and the conditions of the historic moment so clearly demanded that a writer live.

I call the accident that killed Camus a scandal because it showed up, at the heart of the human world, the absurdity of our profoundest exigencies. Camus, suddenly struck down at twenty by a disease that turned his life upside down,[2] discovered the Absurd, that imbecilic negation of mankind. He came to terms with it, he *thought through* his unbearable condition and came through it. And yet we would think that his early works alone tell the truth of his life, since this restored invalid has now been snuffed out by an unforeseeable death from out of the blue. The absurd would be that question no one asks him any more, that he no longer asks anyone, this silence that is no longer even a silence, that is absolutely *nothing* any more.

I do not believe this. As soon as it shows itself, the inhuman becomes part of the human. Every arrested life—even that of such a young man—is *both* a gramophone record being smashed to smithereens and a complete life. For all those who loved him, there is an unbearable absurdity in this death. But we shall have to learn to see this mutilated *oeuvre* as a total one. To the very extent that Camus' humanism contains a *human*

---

2 This is, presumably, a reference to the tuberculosis that he contracted in his youth. [Trans.]

attitude to the death that was suddenly to overtake him, insofar as his proud search for happiness implied and called for the *inhuman* need to die, we shall recognize in this work, and in the life that is inseparable from it, the pure, victorious attempt of a man to reclaim every moment of his existence from his future death.

France-Observateur, 505 (7 January 1960)

*

THE OUTSIDER EXPLAINED

Hardly was Monsieur Camus's *The Outsider* off the presses than it met with enormous acclaim. It was widely said to be 'the best book since the armistice'. Among the literary productions of its time, the novel was itself an outsider. It came to us from the other side of the line, from across the sea. In that bitter coal-less spring, it spoke to us of the sun, not as an exotic marvel but with the weary familiarity of those who have had too much of it. It wasn't concerned to bury the old regime with its own hands once again, nor to din into us the sense of our unworthiness. Reading it, we remembered that there had, in the past, been works that claimed to stand on their own merits and not prove anything. But, as the price to be paid for this arbitrariness, the novel remained rather ambiguous: what were we to make of this character who, the day after his mother had died, 'was swimming in the sea, entering into an irregular liaison and laughing at a Fernandel film', who killed an Arab 'because of the sun' and who, on the eve of his execution, stating that he had 'been happy, and . . . was still happy', wished for crowds of spectators around the scaffold to 'greet [him] with cries of hatred'.[1] Some said: 'he's a poor fool, an idiot'; others, more insightfully: 'he's an innocent.' And yet the sense of that innocence remained to be understood.

In *The Myth of Sisyphus*, which appeared a few months later, M. Camus provided us with an accurate commentary on his work: his hero was neither good nor evil, moral nor immoral. These are not categories that suit him: he is a member of a very peculiar species, for which the author reserves the name '*absurd*'. But, when M. Camus uses it, this term assumes two very different meanings: the absurd is both a state of fact and the lucid consciousness some people acquire of that state. The 'absurd' man is the one who, from a fundamental absurdity, unfailingly draws the inevitable conclusions. There is the same shift in meaning here as when the young people who dance to 'swing' music are called the 'swing generation'. What, then, is the absurd as a state of fact, as an original datum? It is nothing less than man's relation to the world. Primary absurdity is the expression, first and foremost, of a divorce—between man's aspirations towards unity and the insurmountable dualism of mind and nature, between man's longing for the eternal and the *finite* character of his existence, between

1 Albert Camus, *The Outsider* (Joseph Laredo trans.) (London: Penguin Classics, 2000), p. 91, p. 99, p. 117.

the 'concern' that is his very essence and the futility of his efforts. Death, the irreducible pluralism of truths and beings, chance and the unintelligibility of the real—between these poles lies the absurd. To tell the truth, these are not particularly new themes and M. Camus doesn't present them as such. They were enumerated as early as the seventeenth century by a certain sort of hard, terse, contemplative reason that is specifically French: they were commonplaces of classical pessimism. Wasn't it Pascal who stressed 'the natural unhappiness of our feeble, mortal condition, so wretched that nothing can console us when we really think about it'? Wasn't it he who marked out reason's place? Wouldn't he wholly agree with M. Camus when he writes: 'The world is neither (entirely) rational, nor so irrational either'? Didn't he show us that 'custom' and 'distractions' mask man's 'nothingness, his foresakenness, his insufficiency, his dependence, his impotence, his emptiness'? With the frosty style of *The Myth of Sisyphus* and with the subject matter of his essays, M. Camus places himself in the great tradition of those French Moralists whom Charles Andler rightly calls the forerunners of Nietzsche. As for the doubts he raises about the scope of our reason, these are in the most recent tradition of French epistemology. Just think of scientific nominalism, of Poincaré, Duhem and Meyerson,[2] and you will have a better understanding

2 Henri Poincaré (1854–1912) and Pierre Duhem (1861–1916): prominent French mathematicians and philosophers of science; Émile Meyerson (1859–1933): a Polish-born, German-educated, French chemist and philosopher of science. [Trans.]

of the criticism our author makes of modern science: '[Y]ou tell me of an invisible planetary system in which electrons gravitate around a nucleus. You explain this world to me with an image. I realize then that you have been reduced to poetry'.[3] This is expressed separately, but almost at the same moment, by an author who draws on the same sources, when he writes: '(Physics) employs mechanical, dynamical or even psychological models interchangeably, as though, once freed from ontological pretensions, it were becoming indifferent to the classical antinomies of mechanism or dynamism, which presuppose an innate nature.'[4] M. Camus makes a point of citing passages from Jaspers, Heidegger and Kierkegaard, which, in my view, he doesn't always seem clearly to understand. But his real masters are to be found elsewhere. With the turn of his reasoning, the clarity of his ideas, his essayistic style and a certain kind of sunlit, ordered, formal, desolate grimness, everything about him points to a man of classic temperament, a writer of the Mediterranean. Even his method ('Solely the balance between evidence and lyricism can allow us to achieve simultaneously emotion and lucidity'[5]) is redolent of the old 'impassioned geometries' of Pascal and Rousseau, and brings him considerably closer, for example, to

---

3 Albert Camus, *The Myth of Sisyphus* (Justin O'Brien trans.) (London: Penguin, 2005), p. 18.

4 Maurice Merleau-Ponty, *La Structure du Comportement* (Paris: La Renaissance du Livre, 1942), p. 1.

5 Camus, *The Myth of Sisyphus*, p. 3.

Maurras,[6] that other man of the Mediterranean from whom, however, he differs in so many ways, than to a German phenomenologist or a Danish existentialist.

But M. Camus would doubtless grant us all that. In his eyes, originality means taking his ideas to their limits; it is not his concern to make a collection of pessimistic maxims. Admittedly, the absurd is neither in man nor in the world, if we take the two separately. But, since it is of the essence of man to 'be-in-the-world', the absurd is ultimately of a piece with the human condition. It is not in any sense, therefore, to be grasped as a simple notion; a gloomy insight reveals it to us. 'Get up, tram, four hours in the office or factory, meal, tram, four hours of work, eat, sleep, Monday, Tuesday, Wednesday, Thursday, Friday and Saturday, all to the same rhythm,'[7] and then, suddenly, 'the stage-sets collapse' and we arrive at a lucidity bereft of hope. Then, if we are able to reject the sham succour of religions or existential philosophies, we have acquired a number of essential self-evident truths: the world is chaos, 'a divine equivalence born of anarchy' And there is no tomorrow, since we die.

> [I]n a universe suddenly divested of illusions and lights, man feels an alien, a stranger. His exile is without remedy since he is deprived of the memory of a lost home or the hope of a promised land.[8]

6 Charles Maurras (1868–1952): essayist and leader of the extreme Right Action française movement. [Trans.]

7 Camus, *The Myth of Sisyphus*, p. 11 (translation modified).

8 Camus, *The Myth of Sisyphus*, pp. 4–5.

This is because man *is not*, in fact, the world:

> If I were a tree among trees, . . . this life would have a meaning or rather this problem would not arise, for I should belong to this world. I should *be* this world to which I am now opposed by my whole consciousness . . . This ridiculous reason is what sets me in opposition to all creation.[9]

This already in part explains the title of the novel: the outsider is the man standing over against the world. To describe his work, M. Camus could just as easily have chosen the name of a novel by Gissing, *Born in Exile*.[10] The outsider is also the man among men. '[T]here are days when . . . we see as a stranger [*étrangère*] the one we had loved.'[11] In the end, it is myself in relation to myself: in other words, the man of nature in relation to the mind: 'the stranger who at certain seconds comes to meet us in a mirror'.[12]

But this is not all there is to it: there is a passion of the absurd. *Homo absurdus* will not commit suicide: he wants to live, without abdicating any of his certainties, without tomorrows, without hope, without illusions, but without resignation either. *Homo absurdus* affirms

9 Camus, *The Myth of Sisyphus*, pp. 49–50.

10 George Gissing (1857–1903): a prolific Yorkshire-born novelist, his *Born in Exile* (1892) was translated into French by Marie Canavaggia and published in 1932. [Trans.]

11 Camus, *The Myth of Sisyphus*, p. 13.

12 Camus, *The Myth of Sisyphus*, p. 13.

himself in revolt. He confronts death with a passionate attention and that fascination liberates him: he knows the 'divine irresponsibility' of the condemned man. Everything is permitted, since God doesn't exist and we die. All experiences are equivalent; it is just a matter of acquiring as many as possible. 'The present and the succession of presents before a constantly conscious soul is the ideal of the absurd man.'[13] All values crumble before this 'ethics of quantity'; the absurd man, pitched into this world, in revolt and with no one to answer to, has 'nothing to justify'. He is *innocent*. Innocent like those primitives Somerset Maugham writes of, before the arrival of the parson who teaches them Good and Evil, tells them what is permitted and what forbidden.[14] For him, *everything* is permitted. He is innocent as Prince Myshkin,[15] who 'lives in a perpetual present, varied only by smiles and indifference'. An innocent in all senses of the term, and an 'Idiot' too, if you will. And this time we fully understand the title of Camus's novel. The stranger or 'outsider' he wishes to depict is precisely one of those terrible innocents who scandalize a society because they don't accept the rules of its game. He lives among strangers, but for them too he is a stranger. This

---

13 Camus, *The Myth of Sisyphus*, pp. 61–2.

14 William Somerset Maugham (1874–1965): one of the most popular English novelists of his day. Sartre is probably thinking of novels such as *The Moon and Sixpence*, based on the life of Paul Gauguin among the 'primitives' of Tahiti. [Trans.]

15 The central character of Dostoevsky's novel *The Idiot*. [Trans.]

is why some will love him, like Marie, his mistress, who likes him 'because he is odd', and others will detest him for the same reason, like the crowd in the courtroom whose hatred he can immediately feel rising towards him. And we ourselves who are not yet, when we open the book, entirely familiar with the feeling of the absurd, would seek in vain to judge him by our usual standards: for us, too, he is a stranger.

So when you opened the book and read, 'I realized that I'd managed to get through another Sunday, that Mother was now buried, that I was going to go back to work and that, after all, nothing had changed,'[16] the shock you felt was intended. It is the outcome of your first encounter with the absurd. But you were probably hoping that as you went on reading, you would find your sense of unease dissipating, that little by little everything would be cleared up, given a rational foundation, explained. Your hopes were dashed: *The Outsider* is not a book that provides explanations. *Homo absurdus* doesn't explain, he describes. Nor is this a book that furnishes proof. M. Camus merely proposes and doesn't trouble to justify that which is, in principle, unjustifiable. *The Myth of Sisyphus* will teach us how to receive our author's novel. We find in that work the theory of the absurdist novel. Although the absurdity of the human condition is its only subject, it isn't a novel that expounds a message; it doesn't emanate from a 'self-satisfied' system of

16 Camus, *The Outsider*, p. 28.

thought intent only on producing evidence for its position. On the contrary, it is the product of a form of thinking that is 'limited, mortal and in revolt'. It proves, in and of itself, the uselessness of abstract reason:

> The preference [the great novelists] have shown for writing in images rather than in reasoned arguments is revelatory of a certain thought that is common to them all, convinced of the uselessness of any principle of explanation and sure of the educative message of perceptible appearance.[17]

Thus the mere fact of delivering his message in the form of a novel reveals a proud humility on M. Camus's part. Not resignation, but the rebellious recognition of the limits of human thought. Admittedly, he felt he had to provide a philosophical translation of his novelistic message and this is precisely what *The Myth of Sisyphus* does. We shall see below what we are to make of this form of duplication. But the existence of this translation in no way detracts from the arbitrary nature of the novel. The absurdist creator has lost even the illusion that his work is necessary. On the contrary, he wants us to be constantly aware of its contingency. He would like to give it the epigraph: 'might never have been', just as Gide wanted to add at the end of *The Counterfeiters* the message: 'could be continued'. It might not have been,

---

17 Camus, *The Myth of Sisyphus*, pp. 97–8.

like this stone, this stream or this face. It is a present that simply is given, like all the world's presents. It doesn't even have that subjective necessity that artists are wont to claim for their works when they say, 'I simply had to write it; I had to get it out of my system.' This is a theme familiar to us from the Surrealist terrorism, though it is exposed here to the harsh light of classicism: the work of art is merely a leaf torn from a life. It does, indeed, express that life: but it might have not done so. Moreover, everything is equivalent: writing Dostoevsky's *The Demons* or drinking a coffee. M. Camus does not, then, require of his readers that attentive solicitude demanded by the writers who 'have sacrificed their lives to their art'. *The Outsider* is one page of his life. And since the most absurd life must be the most sterile, his novel seeks to be magnificent in its sterility. Art is a useless generosity. But let us not be too horrified by this. Beneath M. Camus's paradoxes, I detect the presence of some very wise remarks by Kant on the 'purposeless purposiveness' of the Beautiful. At any rate, *The Outsider* is there, detached from a life, unjustified, unjustifiable, sterile, instantaneous, already left behind by its author, abandoned in favour of other presents. And this is how we should approach it, as a brief communion between two human beings, the author and the reader, in the absurd and beyond the realm of reason.

This gives us an indication of more or less how we are to view *The Outsider*'s central protagonist. If

M. Camus had wanted to write a novel with a message, it would not have been difficult to show a civil servant lording it over his family, then suddenly gripped by a sense of the absurd, battling with it for a while and finally resolving to live out the fundamental absurdity of his condition. The reader would have been convinced at the same time as his character—and by the same arguments. Or, alternatively, he would have recounted the life of one of those saints of absurdity whom he lists in *The Myth of Sisyphus* and of whom he is particularly fond: the Don Juan, the Actor, the Conqueror, the Creator. This is not what he has done and, even for the reader familiar with the theories of absurdity, Meursault, the hero of *The Outsider*, remains ambiguous. We are, admittedly, assured that he is absurd, and pitiless lucidity is his chief characteristic. Moreover, he is, in more than one respect, constructed in such a way as to provide a concerted illustration of the theories advanced in *The Myth of Sisyphus*. For example, M. Camus writes in this latter work: 'A man is more a man by the things he remains silent about than by the things he says.' And Meursault is an example of this manly silence, of this refusal of idle chatter: '[He was asked] whether he'd noticed that I was at all withdrawn and he simply remarked that I only spoke when I had something to say.'[18] And, indeed, two lines before, the same witness for the defence declared that Meursault 'was a man of the world'. When asked 'what he understood by that . . .

18 Camus, *The Outsider*, p. 89.

he announced that everyone knew what that meant.'[19] Similarly, M. Camus dilates at length on love in *The Myth of Sisyphus*: 'Only by reference to a collective way of seeing for which books and legends are responsible,' he writes, 'do we call what binds us to certain creatures love.'[20] And, in a passage that parallels this one, we read in *The Outsider*: 'A minute later she asked me if I loved her. I told her that it didn't mean anything but that I didn't think so.'[21] From this point of view, the debate that began in the court and in the mind of the reader around the question, 'Did Meursault love his mother?' is doubly absurd. First, as the lawyer says, 'after all, is he being accused of burying his mother or of killing a man?'[22] But, above all, the word 'love' is meaningless. Meursault probably put his mother in the Home because he was short of money and 'they had no more to say to each other.' Probably, too, he didn't go to see her often 'because . . . it meant giving up [his] Sunday—let alone making the effort of going to the bus stop, buying tickets and spending two hours travelling.'[23] But what does this mean? Is he not entirely in the present, wrapped up wholly in his present moods? What we call a feeling is simply the abstract unity and the meaning of discontinuous impressions. I am not constantly thinking

---

19 Camus, *The Outsider*, p. 89.

20 Camus, *The Myth of Sisyphus*, p. 71 (translation modified).

21 Camus, *The Outsider*, p. 38.

22 Camus, *The Outsider*, p. 93.

23 Camus, *The Outsider*, p. 11.

of those I love, but I claim to love them even when I am not thinking of them—and I would be capable of compromising my peace of mind in the name of an abstract feeling, in the absence of any real, immediate emotion. Meursault thinks and acts differently: he wants nothing to do with these great continuous and indistinguishable feelings. Love doesn't exist for him, nor even love *affairs*. Only the present and the concrete counts. He goes to see his mother when he wants to and that is all there is to it. If the desire is present, it will be powerful enough to make him take the bus, since another concrete desire will have sufficient force to make this lazybones run flat out and jump on to a moving lorry. But he always refers to his mother affectionately and childishly as *maman* and he never misses a chance to understand her and identify with her. 'Of love I know only that mixture of desire, affection and intelligence that binds me to this or that creature.'[24] We can see, then, that the *theoretical* side of Meursault's character shouldn't be overlooked. Similarly, many of his adventures are there mainly to bring out some particular aspect of fundamental absurdity. For example, as we have seen, *The Myth of Sisyphus* extols the 'divine availability of the condemned man before whom the prison doors open in a certain early dawn'[25]— and it was to have us savour this dawn and this 'availability' that M. Camus condemned his hero to capital

---

24 Camus, *The Myth of Sisyphus*, p. 71.
25 Camus, *The Myth of Sisyphus*, p. 57.

punishment. 'How had I not seen,' he has him say, 'that nothing was more important than an execution . . . and that, in a sense, it was even the only really interesting thing for a man!'[26] We could quote many more such passages. Yet, this lucid, indifferent, taciturn man is not entirely constructed for the needs of the argument. No doubt, once the character was sketched out, it completed the picture itself; it assumed a substance all its own. And yet Meursault's absurdity appears not to be attained, but given. He is like that, and that is all there is to it. His epiphany will come on the last page, but he had always been living by M. Camus's standards. If there were a grace of the absurd, we should have to say that he has grace. He doesn't seem to ask himself any of the questions that are aired in *The Myth of Sisyphus*; and we don't see him in revolt before he is condemned to death. He was happy, he followed his star, and his happiness doesn't even seem to have known that secret sting to which M. Camus refers several times in his essay and which comes from the blinding presence of death. Even his indifference often seems like indolence, as on that Sunday when he stays at home out of sheer laziness and when he admits that he 'was a little bored'. Thus, even to an absurdist gaze, the character retains an opacity all his own. He is by no means the Don Juan, nor the Don Quixote of absurdity; at many points, we might actually see him as its Sancho Panza. He is there, he exists, and

---

26 Camus, *The Outsider*, p. 109.

we can neither entirely understand him nor judge him. In a word, he lives, and it is fictional density alone that can justify him in our eyes.

Yet we should not see *The Outsider* as an entirely arbitrary work. As we have said, M. Camus makes a distinction between the *feeling* and the *notion* of the absurd. On this, he writes: 'Like great works, deep feelings always mean more than they are conscious of saying . . . Great feelings carry with them their own universe, splendid or abject.'[27] And, a little further on, he adds: 'The feeling of the absurd is not, for all that, the notion of the absurd. It lays the foundations for it, and that is all. It is not limited to that notion.'[28] We might say that *The Myth of Sisyphus* aims to provide us with this *notion* and that *The Outsider* seeks to inspire in us the *feeling*. The order in which the two works appeared seems to confirm this hypothesis. *The Outsider*, published first, plunges us without further ado into the 'climate' of the absurd; the essay follows, casting its light on the landscape. The absurd is a discrepancy, a gap. *The Outsider* will, as a result, be a novel of gaps and discrepancies, of disorientation. Hence its skilful construction: on the one hand, the amorphous, everyday flow of lived reality; on the other, the edifying recomposition of that reality by human reason and discourse. The point is that the reader, having first been brought into the presence of

---

27 Camus, *The Myth of Sisyphus*, p. 9 (translation modified).
28 Camus, *The Myth of Sisyphus*, p. 27.

pure reality, rediscovers it without recognizing it in its rational transposition. This will be the source of the feeling of the absurd or, in other words, of our incapability of *thinking* the events of the world with our concepts and words. Meursault buries his mother, takes a mistress and commits a crime. These various facts are recounted at his trial by the assembled witnesses and explained by the public prosecutor: Meursault will have the impression they are talking about someone else. Everything is so constructed as to lead up suddenly to Marie's outburst. Having given an account framed in terms of human rules in the witness box, she bursts into tears: 'it wasn't like that, there was something else and she was being made to say the opposite of what she thought.'[29] These mirror games have been in common usage since Gide's *Counterfeiters*. This is not where M. Camus's originality lies. But the problem he has to solve will force him to adopt an original literary form. If we are to feel the gap between the prosecutor's conclusions and the actual circumstances of the murder, if, when we close the book, we are to retain the impression of an absurd justice that will never be able to comprehend, nor even ascertain the nature of, the acts it proposes to punish, we have first to have been brought into contact with reality or with one of these circumstances. But, in order to establish that contact, M. Camus, like the public prosecutor, has only words and concepts at his disposal.

---

29 Camus, *The Outsider*, p. 91.

Using words and assembling ideas, he has to describe the world before words. The first part of *The Outsider* could, like a recent book, be called *Translated from Silence*.[30] We touch here on a malady shared by many contemporary writers, the earliest signs of which I see in the work of Jules Renard. I shall call it the obsession with silence. M. Paulhan[31] would certainly see it as an effect of literary terrorism. It has assumed a thousand forms, from the 'automatic writing' of the Surrealists to the famous 'theatre of silence' of Jean-Jacques Bernard. This is because silence, as Heidegger says, is the authentic mode of speech. Only he who knows how to speak can be silent. M. Camus speaks a lot in *The Myth of Sisyphus*. He even chatters. And yet he tells us of his love of silence. He quotes Kierkegaard's phrase, 'The surest of stubborn silences is not to hold one's tongue but to talk.'[32] And he adds, himself, that, 'A man is more a man by the things he remains silent about than by the things he says.' So, in *The Outsider*, he set about being *silent*. But how can one be silent with words? How, with concepts, can one render the unthinkable, disordered succession of present moments? It is a challenge that requires recourse to a new kind of technique.

---

30 The reference is to Joë Bousquet, *Traduit du Silence* (Paris: Gallimard, 1941). [Trans.]

31 Jean Paulhan (1884–1968): a French writer, literary critic and publisher, and director of the literary magazine *Nouvelle Revue Française*. [Trans.]

32 Camus, *The Myth of Sisyphus*, p. 24. Compare also Brice Parain's theory of language and his conception of silence.

What is that technique? 'It's Kafka written by Hemingway,' someone has suggested. I must admit that I don't see Kafka in it. M. Camus's views are wholly down-to-earth. Kafka is the novelist of impossible transcendence. For him, the universe is bristling with signs we do not understand. There is something behind the scenery. For M. Camus by contrast, the human tragedy is the absence of any transcendence.

> I don't know whether this world has a meaning that transcends it. But I know that I do not know that meaning and that it is impossible for me just now to know it. What can a meaning outside my condition mean to me? I can understand only in human terms. What I touch, what resists me—that is what I understand.[33]

There is no question, then, for him of finding arrangements of words that lead us to suspect an indecipherable, inhuman order. The inhuman is merely the disorderly, the mechanical. There is nothing dubious in his work, nothing disquieting, nothing suggested: *The Outsider* presents us with a succession of luminously clear views. If they disorient us, they do so only by their quantity and the absence of any unifying link. Mornings, clear evenings, relentless afternoons—these are his favourite times of day. The perpetual summer of Algiers is his season. There is scarcely any place for night in his universe. If he speaks of it, he does so in the following terms:

---

33 Camus, *The Myth of Sisyphus*, p. 49.

I woke up with stars shining on my face. Sounds of the countryside were wafting in. The night air was cooling my temples with the smell of earth and salt. The wondrous peace of this sleeping summer flooded into me.[34]

The person who wrote these lines is as far as can be from the *Angst* of a Kafka. He is thoroughly calm amid the chaos. The stubborn blindness of nature irritates him certainly, but it also reassures him. Its irrationality is merely a negative factor: *homo absurdus* is a humanist, he knows only the blessings of this world.

The comparison with Hemingway seems more fruitful. There is an obvious affinity of style. In both texts, we find the same short sentences: each refuses to profit from the impetus of the preceding one; each is a new beginning. Every sentence is like a snapshot of an action or an object. Each new action and each new object has its corresponding new sentence. And yet I am not satisfied: the existence of an 'American' narrative technique has, without doubt, assisted M. Camus. But I doubt that it has, strictly speaking, influenced him. Even in *Death in the Afternoon*, which is not a novel, Hemingway retains this jolting mode of narration, which conjures each sentence out of nothingness in a kind of respiratory spasm: the style is the man. We already know that M. Camus has a different style, a ceremonial style. But even in *The Outsider*, he occasionally raises the tone: the sentence then has a broader, continuous flow:

34 Camus, *The Outsider*, p. 116.

The cries of the newspaper sellers in the languid evening air, the last few birds in the square, the shouts of the sandwich sellers, the moaning of the trams high in the winding streets of the town and the murmuring of the sky before darkness spills over onto the port, all these sounds marked out an invisible route which I knew so well before going into prison.[35]

Showing through Meursault's breathless narrative, I glimpse a broader underlying poetic prose, which must be M. Camus's personal mode of expression. If *The Outsider* bears such visible marks of the American technique, that is because there is a deliberate borrowing. Among the instruments available to him, M. Camus has chosen the one that seemed best to fit his purpose. I doubt if he will use it again in his future works.

Let us look more closely at the framework of his narrative. We shall get a clearer idea of his methods.

Men too secrete the inhuman. At certain moments of lucidity, the mechanical aspect of their gestures, their meaningless pantomime make silly everything that surrounds them.[36]

Here, then, is what must first be conveyed: *The Outsider* must put us, from the outset, into 'a state of unease at man's inhumanity'. But what are the particular

---

35 Camus, *The Outsider*, p. 93.
36 Camus, *The Myth of Sisyphus*, p. 13.

occasions that can provoke in us this unease? *The Myth of Sisyphus* gives us an example:

> A man is talking on the telephone behind a glass partition; you cannot hear him but you see his incomprehensible dumb-show; you wonder why he is alive.[37]

This tells us what we need to know. It almost tells us too much, for the example reveals a certain bias on the part of the author. The movements of the man on the phone, whom you cannot hear, are only *relatively* absurd: the fact is that he is part of an incomplete circuit. Open the door, put your ear to the receiver and the circuit is re-established: human activity is senseless no longer. Sincerely, then, we would have to say that there are only relative absurdities—and then only by comparison with 'absolute rationalities'. Yet it is not a question of sincerity, but of art. M. Camus has a ready-made method: he will insert a glass screen between the characters he is talking about and the reader. What could be more inept than men behind a window? The glass seems to let everything through, but it actually cuts out just one thing: the meaning of their actions. All that remains is to choose the window. In this case, it will be the Outsider's consciousness. It is, in fact, a transparent medium: we see everything that it sees. Only it has been so constructed as to be transparent to things and opaque to meanings:

---

37 Camus, *The Myth of Sisyphus*, p. 13.

From that point on everything happened very quickly. The men moved towards the coffin with a pall. The priest, his followers, the warden and myself all went outside. By the door there was a woman I hadn't seen before. 'This is Mr Meursault,' the warden said. I didn't hear the woman's name, I just understood that she was the duty nurse. She bowed her head, without a trace of a smile on her long, bony face. We stood aside to make way for the body.[38]

People are dancing behind a glass screen. Between them and the reader a consciousness has been inserted—almost nothing, a pure translucency, a purely passive thing recording all the facts. But this has done the trick: precisely because it is passive, the consciousness records only the facts. The reader has not noticed the interposing of the screen. But what, then, is the assumption implied by this kind of narrative? In short, a melodic organization has been turned into an assemblage of invariant elements; it is being claimed that the succession of *movements* is strictly identical with the *act* conceived as a totality. Are we not confronted here with the analytic presupposition that all reality is reducible to a sum total of elements? But if analysis is the instrument of science, it is also the instrument of humour. If I want to describe a rugby match and write: 'I saw adults in short trousers fighting and throwing themselves on the ground in an

---

38 Camus, *The Outsider*, p. 19.

effort to get a leather ball through two wooden posts,'
I have summed up what I *saw*; but I have deliberately
omitted its meaning: I have created something humorous.
M. Camus's narrative is analytical and humorous. He
lies—like every artist—because he is claiming to render
raw experience and yet he is slyly filtering out all the
meaningful connections, which are also part of the experience. This is what David Hume did when he announced
that all he could find in experience was isolated impressions. This is what today's American new realists do when
they deny that there is anything between phenomena but
external relations. Contrary to that view, contemporary
philosophy has established that meanings are also immediate data. But that would carry us too far from our
subject here. Let us simply note that the universe of
homo absurdus is the analytical world of the new realists.
In the literary world, this is an approach with a strong
track record. It is Voltaire's approach in *L'Ingénu* and
Micromégas, and Swift's in *Gulliver's Travels*. For the
eighteenth century had its outsiders too—'noble savages'
as a rule, who, when carried off to unfamiliar civiliza-
tions, perceived the facts before they could grasp their
meaning. Wasn't the effect of this discrepancy precisely
to prompt in the reader a sense of absurdity? M. Camus
seems to remember this on several occasions, particularly
when he shows us his hero pondering the reasons for his
imprisonment.[39]

---

39 Camus, *The Outsider*, pp. 76–7.

It is this analytic method that explains the use of the American technique in *The Outsider*. The presence of death at the end of our road has sent our futures up in smoke; there is 'no tomorrow' to our lives; they are a succession of present moments. What does this express, other than that *homo absurdus* applies his analytical spirit to time? Where Bergson saw a form of organization that cannot be broken down into smaller units, *his* eye sees only a series of instants. It is the plurality of the incommunicable instants that will, in the end, account for the plurality of beings. What our author borrows from Hemingway, then, is the discontinuity of his chopped-up sentences, which precisely apes the discontinuity of time. We are now better able to understand the cast of his narrative: each sentence is a present moment. But it is not a vague present that smudges and runs into the following one. The sentence is distinct, crisp, self-contained; an entire void separates it from the next one, just as Descartes's moment is separated from the moment that follows. Between each sentence and the next, the world is annihilated and reborn: as it emerges, the word is a creation *ex nihilo*; a sentence in *The Outsider* is an island. And we tumble from sentence to sentence, from void to void. It is to accentuate the solitude of each sentence unit that M. Camus chose to narrate his story in the present perfect tense.[40] The French past definite is the tense of

---

40 The use of the present perfect in French is quite different from its use in English. In particular, it is used for completed actions in the past, whereas the English present perfect requires almost always

continuity: '*Il se promena longtemps.*' These words refer us to a *plu*perfect, and to a future. The reality of the sentence is the verb, the act, with its transitive character, its transcendence. '*Il s'est promené longtemps*' conceals the verbalness of the verb. The verb here is shattered, broken in two: on the one hand, we find a past participle that has lost all transcendence and is as inert as a thing; on the other, there is the verb 'to be' which functions merely as a copula, joining participle to noun as it might join complement to subject. The transitive character of the verb has vanished and the sentence has become frozen; its reality now is the noun. Instead of projecting itself between past and future, like a bridge, it is merely a little, isolated, self-sufficient substance. If, moreover, one takes care to reduce it as much as possible to the main clause, then its internal structure becomes perfect in its simplicity; and it gains all the more in cohesiveness. It is truly indivisible, an atom of time. Of course, the sentences are not articulated together: they are merely juxtaposed. In particular, all causal relations are avoided, as they would introduce a glimmer of explanation into the narrative and bring an order to its moments that differed in some way from pure succession. Take the following passage:

> A minute later she asked me if I loved her. *I told her that it didn't mean anything but that I didn't think so. She looked sad.* But as we were getting lunch ready, and for no apparent reason,

---

either that an action is continuing into—or is of some continuing relevance to—the present. [Trans.]

she laughed again, so I kissed her. It was at that point that we heard a row break out in Raymond's room.[41]

I have underlined two sentences which, as carefully as possible, conceal a causal link beneath the mere appearance of succession. When it is absolutely necessary to allude to the previous sentence, the words 'and', 'but', 'then' and 'it was at that moment that' are used, all of which suggest only disjunction, opposition or pure addition. The relations between these temporal units are external ones, just like the relations new realism establishes between things. The real appears without being brought on to the scene and disappears without being destroyed. The world collapses and is reborn with each pulse of time. But do not go thinking it generates itself: it is inert. Every activity on its part would tend to substitute fearful powers for the reassuring disorder of chance. A nineteenth-century naturalist would have written, 'A bridge bestrode the river.' M. Camus rejects such anthropomorphism. He will say, 'Over the river there was a bridge.' In this way the thing immediately imparts its passivity to us. It simply *is there*, undifferentiated:

There were four men in black in the room . . . By the door there was a woman I hadn't seen before . . . Outside the gate stood the hearse . . . Next to it stood the funeral director.[42]

---

41 Camus, *The Outsider*, p. 38.
42 Camus, *The Outsider*, p. 19.

It was said of Jules Renard that he would end up writing, 'The hen lays.' M. Camus and many contemporary authors would write, 'There's the hen and she lays.' The fact is that they like things for what they are in themselves; they do not wish to dilute them into the flow of time. 'There is water': this is a little piece of eternity—passive, impenetrable, incommunicable, sparkling. What sensual delight if one can touch it! For *homo absurdus* this is the one and only blessing of this world. This is why the novelist prefers this shimmering of short-lived moments of brilliance, each of which is a delight, to an organized narrative. This is why, in writing *The Outsider*, M. Camus is able to believe he is being silent: his sentences don't belong to the universe of discourse; they have neither ramifications, continuations, nor internal structure. A sentence from the novel might be defined, like Valéry's 'Sylph' as

Unseen, never happened:
The instant of a naked breast
Between two chemises.

The span of time it takes for a silent intuition to emerge covers it very precisely.

Given this state of affairs, can we speak of a totality we might describe as M. Camus's novel? All the sentences in his book are equivalent, as are all the experiences of *homo absurdus*. Each one takes its place in its own right and sweeps the others into the void. As a consequence, however, except in the rare moments when the author betrays his own principles and *makes* poetry, none stands out from the others. Even the dialogues are integrated into the narrative. Dialogue provides a moment of explanation, of meaning: to give it prominence would be to admit that meanings exist. M. Camus shaves it down, summarizes it, expressing it often in indirect style. He denies it any typographical distinction, so that the phrases uttered seem to be events just like any other; they shimmer for a moment and disappear, like a sudden pulse of heat or a sound or a smell. When you begin reading the book, you don't seem to be in the presence of a novel, but rather of a monotonous chanting, of the nasal singing of an Arab. You have the impression that the book will be like one of those tunes Courteline[43] speaks of, which 'drift away and never return' and which stop suddenly without you knowing quite why. Gradually, however, before the reader's very eyes, the work, by its own dynamic, assumes organized form; it reveals the solid substructure that underpins it. There isn't a single useless detail. Not one that isn't taken up again later and put to use. And when we have closed the book, we realize it could not have begun differently, that it could have had no other ending. In the world that is being presented to us as absurd, from which causality has been carefully extirpated, the tiniest incident has weight. Every single one contributes to leading the hero towards the crime and execution. *The Outsider* is a classical work, a work

---

43 Georges Courteline (1858–1929): one of the leading French dramatists in the early decades of the twentieth century. [Trans.]

of order, written about the absurd and against the absurd. Is this entirely what the author intended? I do not know; it is the reader's opinion I am conveying.

And how are we to classify this crisp, clear work—a work that is so carefully put together beneath its apparent disorder, so 'human' and so unsecretive once one has the key to it? We cannot call it a story [*récit*]: the story explains and coordinates as it reproduces events; it substitutes causal order for chronological sequence. M. Camus calls it a 'novel'. Yet the novel requires a continuous flow of time, a development, the manifest presence of the irreversibility of time. Not without some reluctance would I grant that name to this succession of inert present moments, beneath which we can just make out the mechanical economy of a deliberate contrivance. Or we might see it as a *moraliste's* novella, like *Candide* or *Zadig*, with a discreet strain of satire and a series of ironic portraits[44] which, despite what it takes from the German existentialists and the American novelists, is ultimately very much akin to one of Voltaire's tales.

February 1943

---

44 Of the pimp, the investigating magistrate, the public prosecutor, etc.

＊

A NOTE ON SOURCES

'Reply to Albert Camus'

Originally published as 'Réponse à Albert Camus' in *Situations IV* (Paris: Gallimard, 1964), pp. 90–125.

First published in English translation in *Portraits* (London: Seagull Books, 2009), pp. 123–72.

'Albert Camus'

Originally published as 'Albert Camus' in *Situations IV* (Paris: Gallimard, 1964), pp. 126–9.

First published in English translation in *Portraits* (London: Seagull Books, 2009), pp. 173–8.

'*The Outsider* Explained'

Originally published as 'Explication de *L'Étranger*' in *Situations I* (Paris: Gallimard, 1947), pp. 92–112.

First published in English translation in *Critical Essays* (London: Seagull Books, 2010), pp. 148–84.